Age
Is Nothing
Attitude Is
Everything

Age Is Nothing Attitude Is Everything

Peter Stein

Andrews McMeel
Publishing, LLC

Kansas City

For Mom and Dad, whose
attitudes are always an inspiration.

06 07 08 09 10 SDB 10 9 8 7 6 5 4 3 2 1

ISBN-13: 978-0-7407-6152-2
ISBN-10: 0-7407-6152-8

Library of Congress Control Number: 2006923216

www.andrewsmcmeel.com

ATTENTION: SCHOOLS AND BUSINESSES
Andrews McMeel books are available at quantity discounts with bulk purchase for
educational, business, or sales promotional use. For information, please write to:
Special Sales Department, Andrews McMeel Publishing, LLC, 4520 Main Street,
Kansas City, Missouri 64111.

Introduction

Getting older isn't what it used to be. Increasingly, people are coming to realize that aging can be an enriching, fulfilling experience, one that we have far more control over than we used to think. People are doing something about aging. We're eating better, exercising more, and living longer, healthier, and happier lives.

Yet there's more. One essential—perhaps the essential—key to enjoying life as we age is our attitude. Study after study shows that in large part, what makes us feel good about ourselves is literally feeling good about ourselves. Knowing ourselves. Accepting who we are. Honoring our accomplishments and all we have to offer, learn, and enjoy.

Attitude, of course, affects us at every stage of life. But as we age, staying positive becomes even more important. Age Is Nothing: Attitude Is Everything looks at our "seasoned" years with a knowing smile and gives us a gentle nudge to keep on keeping on and continue growing. To have a sense of humor. To live and love well. The beauty of it is we're all in this together, going through the same challenges and changes, supporting, comforting, and laughing with each other. We're not alone.

This little book celebrates our innate ability to live a young-at-heart life. We can individually and collectively choose to use 'em or lose 'em— our muscles, our minds, our dancing shoes. Embracing life, with all its ups and downs, is the best gift we can give ourselves and others. It's a gift that gently reminds us each day that indeed, age is nothing and attitude is everything.

May you live long and well, and be happy.

So what's the big deal about a few extra years?

Regardless of what some people may believe,
we're not getting older,

we're getting hotter.

No matter what our age,
life is a series of high-flying adventures,

staying on top of things,

ups and downs,

and stunning victories.
(Like finishing first. Or finishing at all.
Or just making it to the bathroom!)

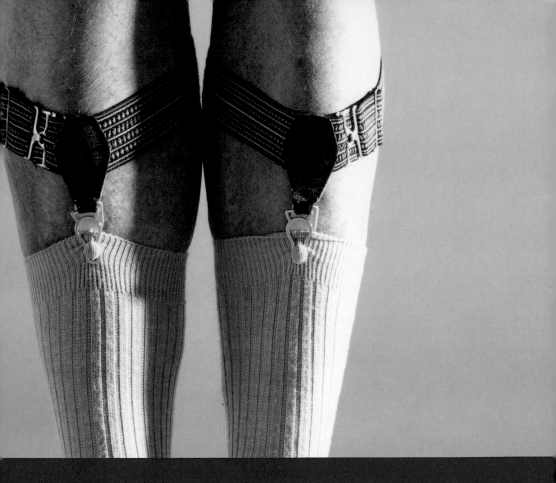

Sure, we could all use a little support
as the years go by,

someone to hug

and a good listener.

Of course it's always smart to start the day
with good feelings.

The truth is, "over the hill" can be,
like, really cool.

Not to mention really *hot.*

We're talking *sizzling* here.

There are definite advantages to getting older.
For instance,

we don't care so much about
what people think of us.

We march to the beat of our own drummer.

We learn to face life in our own unique way

and we don't take no guff from no one.

Yes, we all have our annoying aches and pains,

no matter how hard we try to ignore them.

Still, a positive outlook is important.

So is continuing to stre-e-etch yourself.
A little more . . . and a bit more . . . all the time.

It's also wise to maintain the good ol' friendships from way back.

And don't forget to have a ball!
That way things will keep looking up.

Unless, of course, they're looking sideways.
(And that's okay, too.)

But most important of all,
remember that age is nothing;

attitude is everything.

It doesn't take a genius to know that—

just common sense, and Knowing
that you're more marvelous, more *you* as
you float through life.

So go ahead, get in touch with the kid in you

**and release your inner whippersnapper.
(The good part is you can skip the fake ID.)**

It doesn't matter if you're the cultured type

or a little bit hillbilly.

The main thing is it's never
too late to get a kick out of life.

Let's face it, by the time we reach a certain age,
we all carry around our share of baggage.

That's why it's always important
to express ourselves,

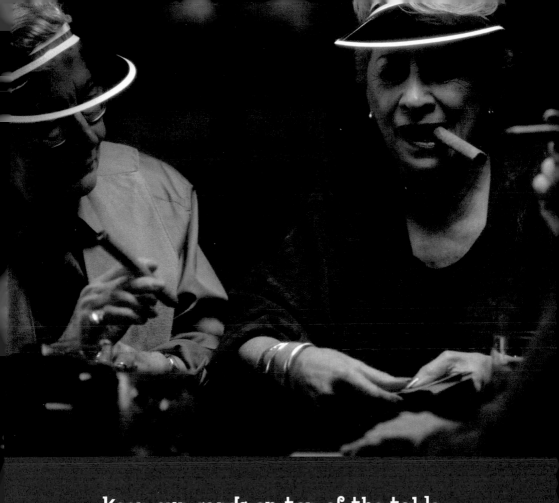

keep our cards on top of the table,

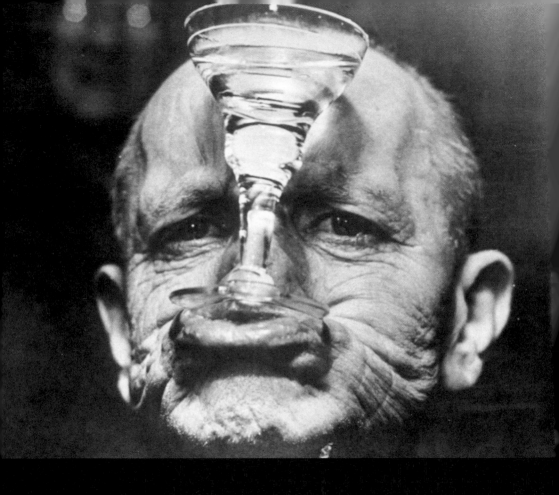

and stay well-balanced.

Though we all know some people
who refuse to see that.

You know the type–they're the ones
whose cups are always half full.

But at five or ninety-five,
you've simply got to give it your best shot.

(Okay, that may be a bit corny,

but it strikes a nice chord, doesn't it?)

So no matter what, stay in the race

and keep a certain amount of drive,

because there's no fairy godmother
to do it for us.

And that's the naked truth.

So if you think that's all just a lot of hot air . . .

if you think for one minute that you're not
amazing, wise, witty, and wonderful . . .

well, you're old enough to know better.

And young enough to dream,

laugh,

love,

and live.